THE UNITED STATES

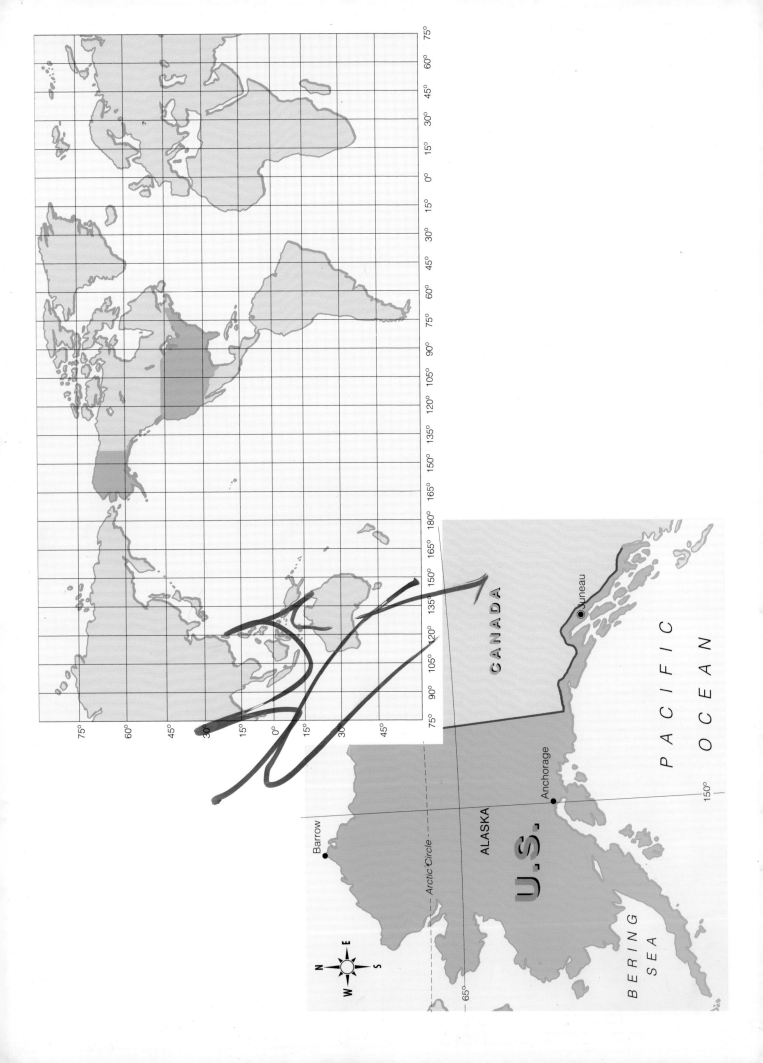

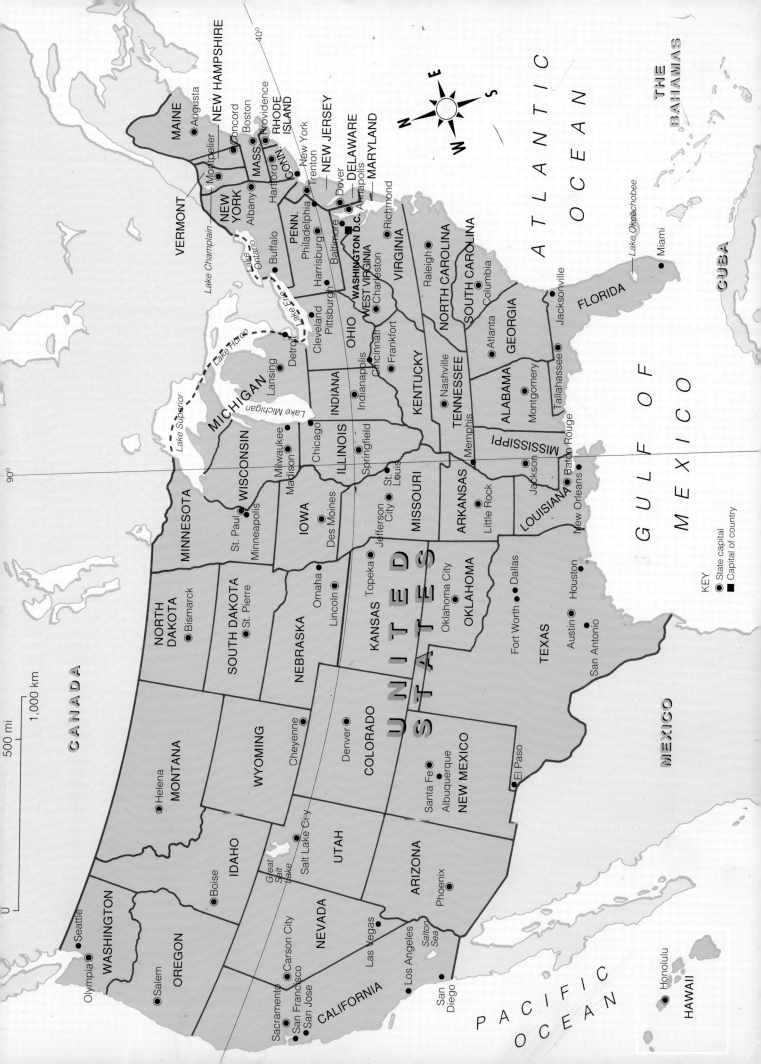

THE
UNITED STATES

John Baines

RAINTREE STECK-VAUGHN
PUBLISHERS

Austin, Texas

Design	Roger Kohn
Editors	Penny Clarke, Helene Resky
DTP editor	Helen Swansbourne
Picture research	Valerie Mulcahy
Illustration	János Márffy
	Coral Mula
Consultant	David Barrs
Commissioning editor	Debbie Fox

We are grateful to the following for permission
to reproduce photographs:
Front Cover: Telegraph Colour Library *above*, Zefa (J. Tobias)
below; Susan Griggs Agency, page 22 (LeRoy Roodson);
Robert Harding Picture Library, pages 11 *below*, 15, 28 *above*,
32, 41; The Image Bank, pages 14 (Co Rentmeester),
17 (Elyse Lewin), 23 (C. L. Chryslin), 25 (Andy Caulfield),
28 *below* (Sobel/Klonsky), 20 (Steve Proehl), 30 (Harald
Sund), 31 (Guido A. Rossi), 35 *above* (Al Satterwhite);
Roger Kohn, page 12; Magnum, pages 8 (Thomas Hoepker),
16 (Burt Clinn), 18 (Alex Webb), 36 (Michael K. Nichols);
42 *below* (Alex Webb); Tony Stone Worldwide, pages 11 *above*
(Tony Craddock), 21 (Mike Powell), 24 (Dennis O'Clair), 26,
27, 35 *below* (John Darling), 37 (Chris Kapolka), 38 (John
Lawlor), 39 (David Hanson); Zefa, pages 8/9, 13, 19, 20, 33
(M. M. Lawrence); Zefa/Allstock, page 42 *above* (C. Krebs).

The statistics given in this book are the most up-to-date
available at the time of going to press

Printed and bound in Hong Kong by
Paramount Printing Group Ltd

1 2 3 4 5 6 7 8 9 0 HK 99 98 97 96 95 94

Library of Congress Cataloging-in-Publication Data
Baines, John D.
The United States / John Baines.
p. cm. – (Country Fact Files)
Includes index.
Summary: Examines the landscape, climate, weather,
population, culture, and industries of the United States.
ISBN 0-8114-1857-X
1. United States – Juvenile literature. [1. United States.]
I. Title. II. Title: United States of America. III. Series.
E156.B34 1994
973–dc20
93-26533
CIP AC

CONTENTS

Words that are explained in the glossary are printed in
SMALL CAPITALS the first time they are mentioned in the text.

⬛ INTRODUCTION

The United States of America is the richest and most powerful country in the world. Only 5 percent of the world's 5.4 billion people are Americans, but most have been influenced by them. For example, one of the U.S.'s best known products, Coca Cola, is sold in over 140 countries.

One of the ways people learn about the United States is through the movies and television programs which are made here. They are shown around the world, usually DUBBED or with subtitles in countries where English is not the main language. People get many impressions of what the U.S.

might be like from them. Depending on what they are watching, it can be the beauty of the countryside, the excitement of football, the crime in the cities, or the tremendous military power of the country.

How accurate are these impressions? This book will help you learn more about the United States, from its scenery to its international trade.

Why is it important to learn about the United States? The United States is both a military and economic power. The U.S. designs and makes the most powerful weapons, and through its military power, it

▲*This home in the rural South is very different from the suburban house (right).*

can protect other countries. It has some of the world's main industrial corporations with factories in many countries, and through its economic power, it influences the economies of other countries. Americans believe in DEMOCRACY and CAPITALISM. Most Americans believe that the American way of life is the best. No country can afford to ignore the United States, although it is sometimes envied because of its wealth and at other times hated because of its power and influence.

THE U.S. AT A GLANCE

- Area: 3,618,770 square miles (9,373,000 sq km)
- Population: 248.7 million (1990 census)
- Density: 68 people per square mile (26.5 people per sq km)
- Capital: Washington, D.C., population 606,900
- Other major cities: New York 7.3 million, Los Angeles 3.4 million, Chicago 2.7 million, Philadelphia 1.5 million, Detroit 1 million, Dallas 1 million, San Francisco 724,000
- Highest mountain: Mt. McKinley, Alaska, 20,318 feet (6,193 m)
- Language: English
- Main religion: Christianity
- Currency: U.S. dollar, written as $
- Economy: Highly industrialized
- Major resources: Coal, oil, minerals, timber, agricultural land
- Major products: Corn, wheat, soybeans, cotton, livestock, automobiles, electrical and electronic goods, coal, oil, gas, iron and steel, minerals, machinery
- Environmental problems: pollution of air, water, and land near industrial areas, soil erosion, deforestation, loss of wilderness

◀ In the United States some people live in large homes in the suburbs.

THE LANDSCAPE

Only Russia, Canada, and China cover larger areas than the United States. The United States is made up of 50 states, although two, Alaska and Hawaii, are separated from the other 48 states. Alaska lies northwest of Canada, partly within the Arctic Circle. Hawaii is a group of subtropical islands in the Pacific Ocean about 2,400 miles (3,862 km) off the Californian coast.

In the east there is a narrow plain along the Atlantic coast. Behind the plain are the Appalachian Mountains with low rounded ridges and shallow valleys.

To the west of the Appalachians the Central Lowlands stretch across to the Rocky Mountains. The lowlands are generally flat or gently rolling and include the Great Plains. The Missouri and Mississippi rivers flow 3,708 miles (5,971 km) from the lowlands into

▲ *The United States is divided into 6 time zones. People on the west coast are 3 hours behind their friends on the east coast.*

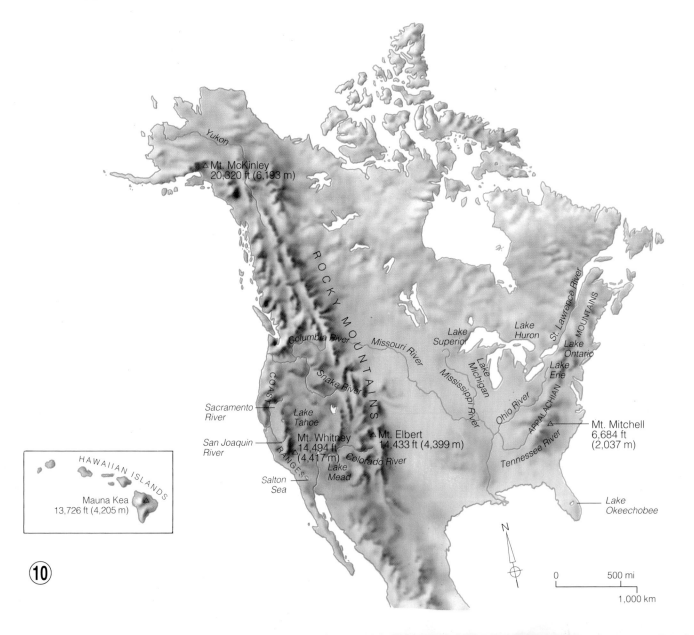

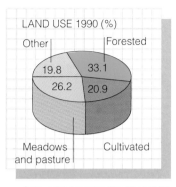

LAND USE 1990 (%)

Other | Forested
19.8 | 33.1
26.2 | 20.9
Meadows and pasture | Cultivated

▲ *The spectacular Grand Canyon in Arizona was cut by the Colorado River. It is 276 miles (445 km) long, 1 mile (1.6 km) deep, and up to 18 miles (29 km) wide.*

▼ *The huge swampy area of Florida called the Everglades is home to many rare species of animals. Part of the Everglades is protected as a national park.*

the Gulf of Mexico through the Mississippi delta. In the northeast are the Great Lakes. Lakes Superior, Huron, Erie, and Ontario are shared with Canada. All of Lake Michigan is in the United States. Niagara Falls is between lakes Erie and Ontario.

The Rocky Mountains rise steeply from the Great Plains, and the peaks are snow covered. To the west are the plateaus and basins with spectacular landforms, such as the Grand Canyon. Along the west coast are the Coast Ranges. These mountains are higher than the Appalachians. They are formed along a zone where two plates of the earth's crust collide. Movements of the plates cause regular earthquakes and volcanic activity. A huge earthquake in 1906 destroyed much of San Francisco. In 1989 another earthquake caused much damage in the San Francisco Bay area.

How warm places are depends on their distance from the equator, distance from the sea, and height above sea level. In Barrow, Alaska, which is near the Arctic Circle, the average daily temperature only rises above freezing point for three months a year. In Miami, Florida, close to the tropics, the average temperature in January is 64°F (18°C).

Temperatures decrease with altitude. In California you can sunbathe on the beach in the morning and then go skiing in the Sierra Nevada mountains only 124 miles (200 km) away.

The difference between the summer and winter temperatures is greater inland than on the coast. The difference at New Orleans, 31 miles (50 km) from the Gulf of Mexico, is 29°F (16°C). In Chicago, 621 miles (1,000 km) from the sea, the range is 50°F (28°C).

Differences in precipitation (rainfall, sleet, and snow) are just as great. Warm winds blowing from the Pacific Ocean bring about 59 inches (150 cm) of rain to the states of Oregon and Washington. Once the winds reach the Great Plains, they are dry and rainfall is only about 16 inches (40 cm). The interior gets most of its rain in summer when warm moist winds are drawn in from the Gulf of Mexico.

Much of the southwestern United States is a desert. Phoenix, Arizona, has less than 1 inch (2 cm) of rain a year. The cold tundra areas of the north are also very dry.

San Francisco is known for its fog, which forms when warm air from the land moves out over the cool sea. The same happens off the coast of New England.

Many parts of the United States are affected by extreme climate and weather conditions. Drought is one example. The Midwest has suffered through serious droughts this century, the last in the late 1980s when farmers lost most of their crops. In 1993 the Midwest had one of the worst floods of this century. Farmers suffered the most losses. Hurricanes are another problem. They are huge tropical storms that strike the south and east coasts. Inland, there are storms called tornadoes, or "twisters," because the air spirals upward sucking dust and debris with it.

▼ *The warm, wet subtropical climate of Hawaii encourages luxuriant plant growth.*

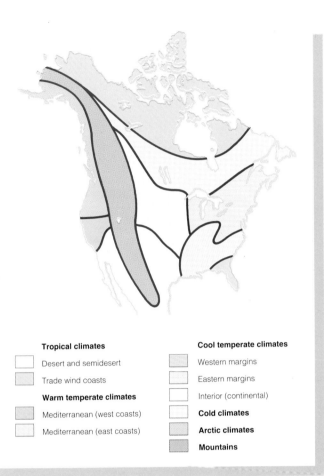

Tropical climates

☐ Desert and semidesert

▦ Trade wind coasts

Warm temperate climates

▨ Mediterranean (west coasts)

☐ Mediterranean (east coasts)

Cool temperate climates

▦ Western margins

▦ Eastern margins

☐ Interior (continental)

Cold climates

▨ Arctic climates

▨ Mountains

▲ *Within the United States are some of the coldest, hottest, driest, wettest, and windiest places on Earth.*

▲ *Lakes in Alaska freeze over during the long, cold winters, but fishermen make holes through the ice to catch fish.*

KEY FACTS

● In the deserts the temperature can rise to 122°F (50°C) during the daytime and fall to freezing point during the night.
● Wind speeds in tornadoes or "twisters" can reach over 186 mph (300 kph).
● It is so cold over most of Alaska that only the top of the ground thaws in summer.

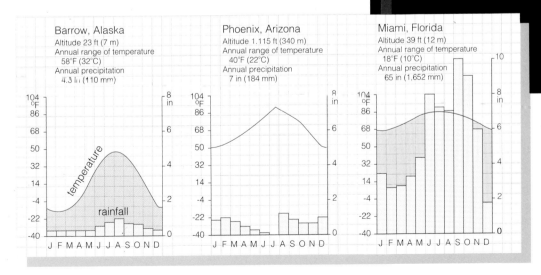

Barrow, Alaska
Altitude 23 ft (7 m)
Annual range of temperature
58°F (32°C)
Annual precipitation
4.3 in (110 mm)

Phoenix, Arizona
Altitude 1,115 ft (340 m)
Annual range of temperature
40°F (22°C)
Annual precipitation
7 in (184 mm)

Miami, Florida
Altitude 39 ft (12 m)
Annual range of temperature
18°F (10°C)
Annual precipitation
65 in (1,652 mm)

◀ *Florida's warm winters are popular with tourists. Barrow is very cold and Phoenix is dry.*

NATURAL RESOURCES

The United States is very rich in natural resources. It has large supplies of timber, fuels, and minerals. However, consumption of resources is so high that supplies of some have to be imported.

Most of the 18 billion cubic feet (532 million m³) of timber cut down in the U.S. each year comes from the mountain areas of the Northwest. Conservationists criticize the timber industry for clearing large areas of trees, not replanting fast enough, and removing ancient forests. Alaska also has an important timber industry.

Oil and gas are found in several states including Pennsylvania, Kentucky, Oklahoma, Kansas, Texas, Louisiana, California, and Alaska. After Russia, the United States is the biggest producer of both oil and gas. So great is the demand for oil that it is mined in such isolated areas as around Prudhoe Bay on the north Alaskan coast. A pipeline has been built 795 miles (1,280 km) across Alaska to Valdez on the south coast to take the oil to a port that is not blocked by ice in winter.

The other major fuel is coal. Almost 980 million tons are mined a year, and 106 million tons are exported. The oldest mining areas are in the Appalachians and to the south of the Great Lakes. More recently mines have been opened in the Rocky Mountains and the northern Great Plains. Although this coal is of a lower quality it is less expensive to mine and contains less sulfur. Sulfur is released

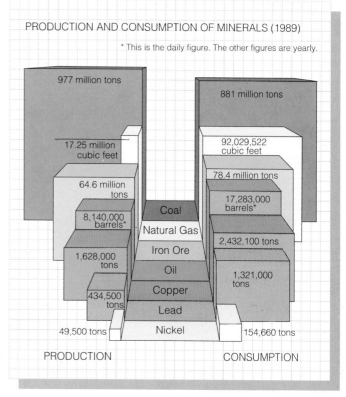

PRODUCTION AND CONSUMPTION OF MINERALS (1989)

* This is the daily figure. The other figures are yearly.

PRODUCTION		CONSUMPTION
977 million tons	Coal	881 million tons
17.25 million cubic feet	Natural Gas	92,029,522 cubic feet
64.6 million tons	Iron Ore	78.4 million tons
8,140,000 barrels*	Oil	17,283,000 barrels*
1,628,000 tons	Copper	2,432,100 tons
434,500 tons	Lead	1,321,000 tons
49,500 tons	Nickel	154,660 tons

◄ STRIP MINES *like this at Gillette, Wyoming, can produce coal cheaply but they damage the environment unless the land is restored afterward.*

into the atmosphere when coal is burned. It is a major cause of acid rain.

Mineral ores are used to supply industry with metals. Iron ore is mined from the hills around the western shores of Lake Superior. Although almost 65 million tons are mined in the United States, the country uses over 78 million tons. Most of this iron ore is imported from Canada and South America.

Many other ores are mined to produce copper, aluminum, lead, zinc, silver, platinum, and gold. Most of the mines are in the mountain areas of the West.

▲A giant sequoia in the Mariposa Grove near Yosemite in California. You can walk though the tree's trunk.

KEY FACTS

● The tallest redwood tree is 367 feet (112 m) high.
● The world's first offshore oil wells were built in the Gulf of Mexico in 1938.
● Alaska is so cold that the oil in the pipeline between Prudhoe Bay and Valdez has to be heated so it will flow easily.
● Coal trains up to 1 mile (1.5 km) long carry 11,020 tons of coal at a time.
● The Bingham Canyon Copper Mine in the Rocky Mountains has excavated a hole almost 2 miles (3 km) across and 2,247 feet (700 m) deep.
● Americans use twice as much energy today as 30 years ago.

NATIVE AMERICANS

Five hundred years ago, the area that is now the United States was occupied by little more than a million people. These Native Americans were descendants of people who had migrated from Asia about 20,000 years earlier. The Inuit (or Eskimos as they used to be called) live in the cold northern areas. Those living in the mainland area are known as American Indians. Originally, there were many tribes of Native Americans, such as the Apache, Navajo, and Sioux. Many Native Americans were killed or died from diseases brought to North America by European settlers. Europeans also greatly changed the Native American way of life. Today there are about 248 million Americans but only 2 million Native Americans.

IMMIGRATION

Many Americans are descended from European immigrants. Place names often indicate which countries these early settlers came from. In the Northeast there are English-sounding place names, such as New Hampshire, New York, and Boston. In the South there are French names, such as New Orleans and Baton Rouge, and in California, Spanish names, such as Los Angeles and San Francisco. Although English is the official language, it is not the first language for 20 percent of the population. Cities like Miami are almost bi-lingual with English and Spanish spoken.

Blacks or African Americans form about 12 percent of the population. They are the largest minority group. Some are descendants of the slaves who were brought from West Africa to work in the plantations of the South. After the abolition

▼ *The Statue of Liberty in New York symbolized for millions of immigrants a country in which they could be free.*

of slavery, many African Americans moved north to find employment in large cities like Detroit, Washington, D.C., New York, and Chicago. Hispanics are the second largest minority group. They form about 7 percent of the population.

During the 1970s, 1.6 million people came from Asia alone to settle in the United States. Immigration today is more carefully controlled, and only about half a million people a year are allowed to settle in the United States.

KEY FACTS

● There were 4 million slaves in the U.S. at the time of the Civil War, 1861–1865.
● Forty-three million people live in the north-eastern MEGALOPOLIS.
● Between 1900 and 1910, 8.8 million immigrants came to the U.S.
● The Sears Tower in Chicago is the highest building in the U.S. It has 110 floors and is 1,454 feet (443 m) high. It uses as much electricity as a town of 150,000 people.
● A Dutch trading company purchased Manhattan from the Native Americans in 1626 and called it New Amsterdam.

▲*Although their ancestors came from many different parts of the world, these children are all Americans.*
▼*At the ceremony to become a U.S. citizen all immigrants say: "I pledge allegiance to the flag of the United States of America and to the Republic for which it stands, one nation under God indivisible with liberty and justice for all."*

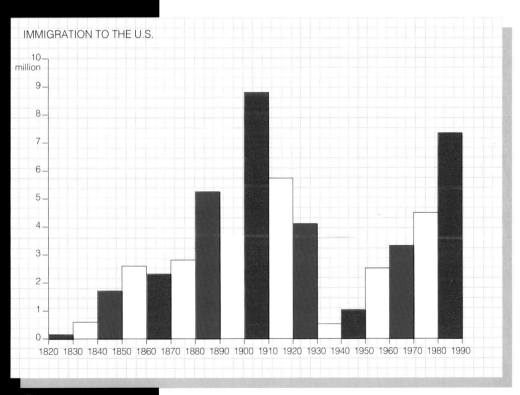

IMMIGRATION TO THE U.S.

◀ *Two-thirds of Native Americans live on reservations where their traditional culture is often linked with contemporary American culture.*

▼ *Indian reservations in the United States*

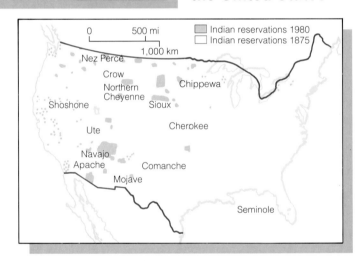

		Indian reservations 1980
0	500 mi	Indian reservations 1875
	1,000 km	

Nez Percé
Crow
Northern Cheyenne
Chippewa
Shoshone
Sioux
Ute
Cherokee
Navajo
Apache
Comanche
Mojave
Seminole

URBAN AMERICA

Three-quarters of Americans live in cities. There are three areas where the cities have grown so large that they form a huge megalopolis where one city merges into the next. The first stretches between Boston and Washington, D.C. and includes the largest city, New York. Although the area only covers 2 percent of the United States, 20 percent of Americans live in it. The second area is where many industries grew up in the 19th and early 20th centuries. It stretches between Chicago and Pittsburgh. The third stretches between San Francisco and San Diego. This is a newer area and has fewer cities but vast areas of suburbs sprawl over the landscape.

The street pattern in most American cities is like a grid. In New York all the roads called "avenues," like Madison Avenue and Fifth Avenue, go north to south and the streets go east to west.

Although people work in the city, many prefer to live in the suburbs and commute daily. This causes traffic congestion and air pollution. In many cities, sections of older houses and apartments have become run down. The housing conditions in the ghettoes can be appalling with some people living in condemned buildings and many others living on the streets as homeless. Unemployment and crime is high in many cities. Some companies have moved to more pleasant surroundings in the nearby suburbs.

Americans are working to solve the problems in the cities. For example, Boston has worked hard to provide a pleasant and safe environment for people. As a result,

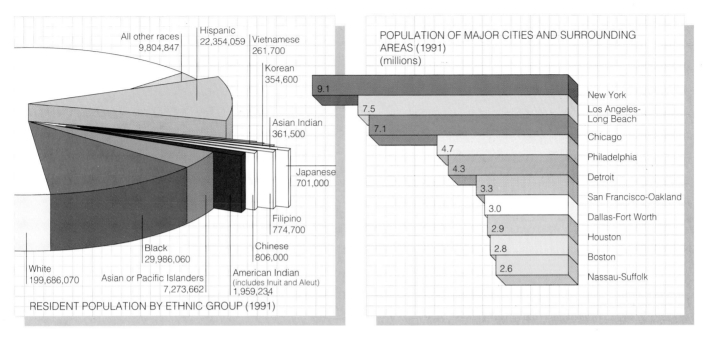

All other races
9,804,847

Hispanic
22,354,059

Vietnamese
261,700

Korean
354,600

Asian Indian
361,500

Japanese
701,000

Filipino
774,700

Chinese
806,000

Black
29,986,060

White
199,686,070

Asian or Pacific Islanders
7,273,662

American Indian
(includes Inuit and Aleut)
1,959,234

RESIDENT POPULATION BY ETHNIC GROUP (1991)

POPULATION OF MAJOR CITIES AND SURROUNDING AREAS (1991)
(millions)

9.1	New York
7.5	Los Angeles-Long Beach
7.1	Chicago
4.7	Philadelphia
4.3	Detroit
3.3	San Francisco-Oakland
3.0	Dallas-Fort Worth
2.9	Houston
2.8	Boston
2.6	Nassau-Suffolk

new businesses have moved into Boston and the city center has prospered.

RURAL LIVING

Although most of the land in the United States is considered to be rural, the population in rural areas is very low. Many Americans who live in rural areas make their living farming, mining, or in businesses related to agriculture. People who move to rural communities are attracted by the lower crime rates and reduced pollution that come with living in the countryside. Social events include family gatherings, church and school activities, clubs, and fairs. There are wealthy, middle-class, and poor people living in rural areas, although the differences among these economic classes are not as great as they are in the cities. Most people who live in rural areas live in single-family houses.

▶ *Telluride in Colorado is typical of the many small towns that are found across the United States. These small towns often include a main street with a few shops and offices.*

FAMILY LIFE

American families are generally small and, compared with most other countries, very well off. Although many American families fit the popular image of the middle-class family, consisting of a mother, father, and two children, there are also single-parent families, couples without children, and people unmarried, widowed, or divorced living on their own. One-quarter of all American children live with one parent. This is because the divorce rate is high with almost one in two marriages ending in divorce.

The average income per head is $19,815, about fifty times that of a country like Pakistan. Half of all young mothers go out to work. Most homes have electricity, refrigerators, and televisions. There are two radios for every person, one television to 1.2 people, and one telephone to 1.3 people. With 1 car to every 1.8 people, the U.S. has the highest car ownership in the world. The average working week is 41 hours, higher than in most developed countries but less than in underdeveloped countries.

RELIGIOUS DAYS AND HOLIDAYS	
January 1	New Year's Day
January 15	Martin Luther King Day
Third Monday in February	Presidents' Day
May 28	Memorial Day
July 4	Independence Day
First Monday in September	Labor Day
October 12	Columbus Day
November 11	Veterans' Day
Fourth Tuesday in November	Thanksgiving
December 25	Christmas Day

EDUCATION

Families consider education to be very important. Each state is responsible for providing schooling. In general, school is compulsory between the ages of 5 and 16. However, 95 percent of all 5- and 6-year-olds go to school, and 34 percent of 18- to 24-year-olds attend colleges and universities. Equal numbers of young men and women stay in school beyond the compulsory school age. Women have more formal education than men, but only 3 percent of top managers are women.

◀ *Families sometimes tour the many state and national parks in campers and mobile homes.*

KEY FACTS

● Eighty-three percent of American homes are detached.

● Twelve percent of Americans are over age 65. In Miami, 17% of the population is over 65 because many move there when they retire.

● The Astrodome in Houston, Texas, which seats almost 55,000 people, is large enough to accommodate baseball and football games.

● There are over 9,600 radio stations, 1,092 television stations, and 1,611 daily newspapers.

● The average American viewer is likely to see 15 murders a week on television.

▲*Many Americans enjoy professional sports, such as football. Fans follow their teams fervently, hoping to see them play in the Super Bowl.*

Children study a wide variety of subjects. Schools today are emphasizing the variety of cultures found in the United States. Some children are bused out of their neighborhood so that schools can have mixed ethnic groups. The public education system is paid for through local taxes. But about 11 percent of children go to private schools where a tuition is paid.

There are many outstanding colleges and universities. Some of the oldest, such as Harvard (1636) and Yale (1701), are located in New England.

◀ *Some buildings in the inner city have fallen into disrepair. Employment is hard to find, and crime and drug abuse are common.*

SOCIAL PROBLEMS

Like most industrialized countries, the United States has many social problems. These problems keep people from meeting their needs.

Some problems are linked to poverty. Approximately 13.5 percent of the population lives below the poverty level. Many poor people live in the big cities. Living conditions in poorer parts of the cities are sometimes inferior.

Unemployment is another social problem in the United States. The unemployment rate has reached 7.8 percent, the highest it has been in 8 years. More than 3 million people are receiving unemployment benefits.

The United States has a high cost of living. Prices for goods and services have increased. This means that some Americans cannot afford to buy some of the goods and services that they need.

The American education system has also been criticized. Some people feel that young Americans are not getting the education they need in order to become good citizens.

Many Americans have made a strong commitment to try to solve these problems. Through government and local efforts, people in the United States are trying to make changes that will make life better for everyone.

PERCENTAGE OF HOMELESS PEOPLE (1990) (%)

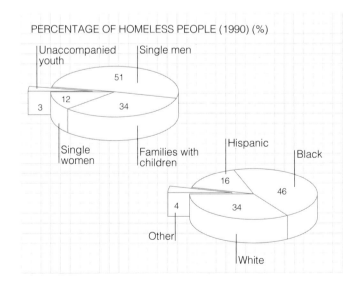

►*Yellow school buses, like those in the picture, are used to take children to and from school every day.*

LEISURE

Americans enjoy watching and participating in many sports, including basketball, baseball, and football. Baseball is the most popular sport, and about 53 million people a year go to watch games. Millions more watch them on television. Many Americans, especially in the Southwest, enjoy rodeos where cowboys show their skills.

A favorite leisure activity in the U.S. is watching television. There are about 1,000 TV stations, although most are local rather than national. Viewers have more choices than anywhere else in the world.

Americans enjoy eating out. They also appreciate convenience. The United States introduced the world to fast food through large food chains.

More Americans are becoming more health conscious. They are jogging, joining health clubs, and eating more healthily.

RELIGION

Eighty-seven percent of people say they are Christian, and 40 percent go to church regularly. Churches run 200 television stations and 3 networks, and their programs are seen by 60 million people a week. Other religions represented are Jewish (2.7%), Muslim (1.9%), and Hindu (0.2%).

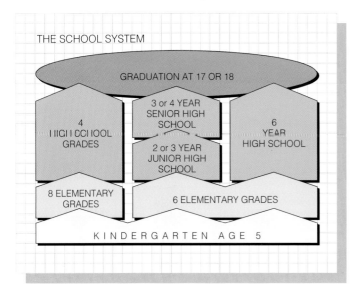

THE SCHOOL SYSTEM

GRADUATION AT 17 OR 18

3 or 4 YEAR SENIOR HIGH SCHOOL

4 HIGH SCHOOL GRADES

6 YEAR HIGH SCHOOL

2 or 3 YEAR JUNIOR HIGH SCHOOL

8 ELEMENTARY GRADES

6 ELEMENTARY GRADES

KINDERGARTEN AGE 5

◄ *Education is the responsibility of each state. However, the curriculum is very similar throughout the country.*

In 1776 thirteen British colonies in North America declared they were the independent nation called the United States of America. In 1781, led by George Washington, they won the American War of Independence against Great Britain. In 1789 the Constitution that remains to this day was written and approved.

Other states joined the original thirteen, but, between 1861 and 1865, the Civil War nearly divided the country because the states in the South wanted to continue with slavery, but the North wanted to abolish it. The North won, and slavery was abolished.

Each state has its own government which makes its own laws relating to taxes, law courts, the police force, and education. The laws must not contradict the Constitution of the United States. The people elect a

▲*The White House in Washington, D.C., is the president's home and office. Washington, D.C., became the capital and seat of government in 1800.*

KEY FACTS

● George Washington was the first President of the U.S.A.
● The "D.C." in Washington, D.C., stands for District of Columbia.
● About 600,000 people were killed in the Civil War.
● The United States bought Alaska from Russia in 1867.
● The U.S. is home to the United Nations and many of its agencies, including the World Bank.

▶ *The two main political parties spend millions of dollars on campaigning. They use all the modern media techniques, including television advertising. The big presidential rallies sometimes resemble a Hollywood extravaganza.*

GOVERNMENT OF THE U.S.

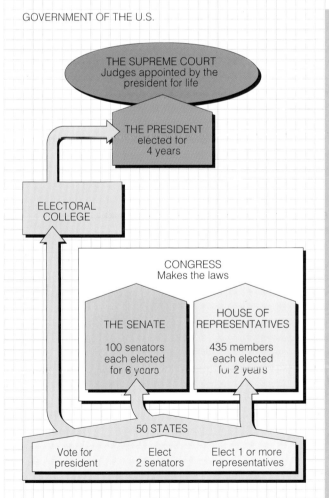

THE SUPREME COURT
Judges appointed by the president for life

THE PRESIDENT
elected for
4 years

ELECTORAL
COLLEGE

CONGRESS
Makes the laws

THE SENATE

100 senators
each elected
for 6 years

HOUSE OF
REPRESENTATIVES

435 members
each elected
for 2 years

50 STATES

| Vote for president | Elect 2 senators | Elect 1 or more representatives |

◀ **The U.S. government is headed by the president. He is responsible for carrying out the laws of the land.**

governor and representatives to make the laws.

National laws are made by the U.S. Congress. Congress is made up of the Senate and the House of Representatives. Each state elects two senators to the Senate and one or more representatives, depending on the population of the state, to the House of Representatives.

The Supreme Court is the most important court of law in the country. The Court makes sure that no laws contradict the Constitution.

The American people elect the president through the Electoral College. A candidate wins the electoral votes in a state by winning the state's popular vote.

There are two main parties: the Republicans and the Democrats. They nominate candidates for election. In national elections, voters can choose the candidates.

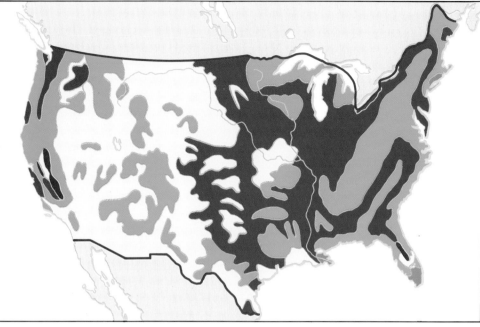

▶ Farming varies considerably across the U.S. because of the many different climate and soil conditions.

Key:
- Arable
- Fruit and vegetables
- Grazing
- Forest with arable and pasture
- Nonagricultural land

Farming in the U.S. is very efficient. Not only can farmers produce enough food for everyone, they also export it to other countries. Farm products account for about 10 percent of American exports. The U.S. produces 14 percent of the world's wheat and 46 percent of its corn. However, this huge production only employs 3 percent of the labor force because farmers use the latest agricultural machinery and chemicals.

In Florida the subtropical climate is ideal for growing citrus fruits, such as oranges. Florida produces one-third of all citrus fruits in the U.S. Oranges are Florida's most important crop, and most are made into orange juice. Oranges for eating usually come from California.

Another important crop is cotton. Cotton is grown in all the southern states from California to South Carolina, but it is no longer as common as it used to be. Other crops, such as soybeans, are now grown.

The main food-producing area lies in the north between the Rocky Mountains and the Appalachians. South of the Great Lakes

▼ The huge flat fields of Minnesota are ideal for big machines. These combine harvesters can cut enough wheat in an hour to feed a family for 40 years.

FOOD INTAKE IN CALORIES PER DAY	
U.S.	3,642
Belgium	3,850
Germany	3,800
U.K.	3,257
Japan	2,858
China	2,628
India	2,204
Bangladesh	1,922

▲*These water sprinklers mean the desert can grow crops. The sprinklers move around in circles. From the air, these irrigated areas stand out as huge green circles.*

developing wheat that will grow fast and not die if there is too little rain, production has increased. The U.S. exports about 33 million tons of wheat a year.

The main ranching areas are farther west, stretching from North Dakota to Texas where it is too dry for growing certain crops. It was from this area that the legends of the Wild West developed. Today "producers" rear calves on the Plains and sell them to "feeders" who fatten them up in huge pens ready for slaughter. Meat is an important part of the American diet, whether it is a thick steak or a hamburger.

Central Valley in California has become the main region for producing fruit, flowers, and vegetables, although the area hardly receives any rainfall. All the major rivers flowing into the Sacramento and San

corn is the main crop, usually grown in rotation with soybeans. About 90 percent of the corn is fed to animals. The area produces half of all the pigs in the U.S.

To the west, more wheat is grown. The climate is really too dry and the summers too short for growing wheat, but by

◄ *Californian wines are famous throughout the world. Napa Valley is one of the main grape-growing areas.*

▼ *Tending the vines is still best done by people, though machines sometimes pick the grapes.*

Joaquin rivers are dammed. The water moves through a network of canals to irrigate an area that is semidesert. Products are sent to most parts of the U.S.

In Alaska, where the climate is too harsh for growing crops, fishing is very important. But the numbers of fish have declined because too many have been caught.

KEY FACTS

● Americans eat about 110 pounds (50 kg) of meat a year compared with 50 pounds (23 kg) eaten by Europeans.
● Almost half of the fruit and vegetables produced in the U.S. comes from California.
● The U.S. produces 8 million tons of oranges a year.
● The U.S. has 1,550 million chickens, 99 million cattle, and 55.5 million pigs.
● One Alaskan specialty is the king crab, which measures 6.5 feet (2 m) from claw to claw.

TRADE AND INDUSTRY

◄ **San Francisco has one of the most picturesque harbors in the world. The Golden Gate Bridge spans the entrance to the San Francisco Bay.**

The industries of the United States and Japan each produce twice as much as Germany, the third-highest producer.

MANUFACTURING INDUSTRY
Industry has always been important to Americans. Importing goods was expensive, and the country had a wealth of minerals and energy supplies that it could use to make products for itself. The American flair for enterprise has helped the growth of industry. Alexander Graham Bell invented the telephone and now all countries have telephone systems. Henry Ford introduced

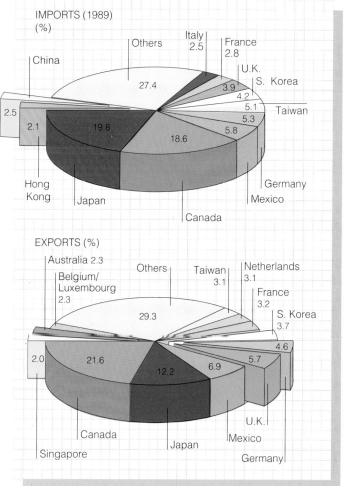

IMPORTS (1989) (%)

Others 27.4
China 2.5
Italy 2.5
France 2.8
U.K. 3.9
S. Korea 4.2
Taiwan 5.1
5.3
Germany 5.8
2.1
Japan 19.8
Canada 18.6
Hong Kong
Mexico

EXPORTS (%)

Australia 2.3
Belgium/ Luxembourg 2.3
Others 29.3
Taiwan 3.1
Netherlands 3.1
France 3.2
S. Korea 3.7
4.6
2.0
Canada 21.6
Japan 12.2
6.9
5.7
Singapore
U.K.
Mexico
Germany

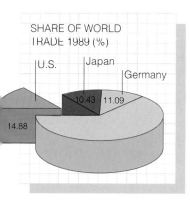

SHARE OF WORLD TRADE 1989 (%)

U.S. 14.88
Japan 10.43
Germany 11.09

◄ **The U.S. is the world's biggest trading nation.**

► **The U.S. trades with most countries.**

KEY FACTS

● Boeing, based in Seattle, produces half of all the world's airliners.
● Columbia Pictures is now owned by a Japanese company.
● *Robin Hood, Prince of Thieves* cost $55 million to make and in the U.S. alone made $165 million in the first year.
● In 1989 American factories produced 24.8 million television sets, 10.8 million vehicles, 10.5 million microwave ovens, 7 million refrigerators and 6.2 million washing machines.

▲*The U.S. is the main supplier of aircraft to the world's airlines. This factory at Everett, Washington, produces Boeing aircraft – the world's most popular passenger planes.*

the first assembly line to build his cars more cheaply, and now most goods are produced in this way. American industries are world leaders in many areas, including aerospace, microelectronics, and medicines. Manufacturing employs about 19 million people, more than a quarter of all working people.

One of the most important products a wealthy industrial country needs is steel. It is used by the building, engineering, and manufacturing industries. The U.S. produces about 108 million tons a year compared with 117 million tons in Japan and 21 million tons in Great Britain. Almost 10 percent of the production comes from the plant on Sparrow's Point on the Chesapeake Bay. Most other plants are in

the region between Pittsburgh and Chicago where good transportation facilities bring together the two raw materials needed to make steel: coal and iron ore.

The Midwest is also the main manufacturing region. It produces consumer goods, like stoves and freezers, but the single most important industry is the manufacture of vehicles and vehicle parts. Detroit is nicknamed "Motor Town" or "Motown," although many cars are now assembled in other parts of the country from parts made in the Detroit area.

The principal industries in the U.S. have changed over the years. At the beginning of the century, the main industries were textiles, clothing, tobacco, leather, products made from oil, making metals, like iron and steel, and making transportation equipment. Many of these American industries have found it difficult to compete with goods made in Asia, especially in Japan, Taiwan, and South Korea. For example, the number of imported cars has risen from just over 2 million in 1970 to almost 4.5 million a year today — more than half of all new cars. Many factories have closed, giving the north eastern and midwestern regions the name of "the rust belt." Unemployment is high.

High-tech industries, such as micro-electronics, are the fastest-growing industries today. They are bringing about the dawn of the new information age. The area between San Francisco Bay and the Santa Cruz Mountains has become known as Silicon Valley because all along Highway 280 there are factories developing and manufacturing components for all types of computers and computer-controlled equipment. The silicon chip is the basis of these industries.

The area around the Gulf of Mexico is also an important industrial area, especially for oil refining and chemicals. Since the space program set up its headquarters in Houston, Texas, many new computer and aerospace industries have developed there. For example, rockets are made in New Orleans and taken to Cape Canaveral in Florida for launching.

USING ENERGY

Americans use large amounts of energy, especially energy from oil. The average American consumes almost twice as much energy as the average European. Some experts say that supplies will only last another 50 years at most, so industry needs to find alternative sources of energy. Hydroelectric power provides about 9 percent and nuclear power 17 percent of electrical power. Even wind and solar power are being used, but they contribute only small amounts of energy. For example, the wind farms in California only provide 1 percent of the electrical energy needed by the state.

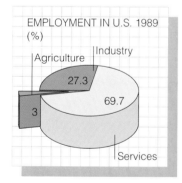

EMPLOYMENT IN U.S. 1989 (%)

Agriculture 3
Industry 27.3
Services 69.7

▶ *This oil refinery in Texas is typical of many around the Gulf of Mexico.*

AMERICAN COMPANIES

Many companies that originated in the U.S. have become household names all around the world including Coca Cola, Pepsi, McDonald's, Pizza Hut, IBM, Kodak, Ford, General Motors, Paramount, Hoover, Exxon, and Texaco. The largest American company is General Motors, which sold goods worth $126 billion in 1990.

There are also many small businesses in the U.S. They are very important to the economy and employ about half of all American workers. Many of these businesses are franchises. A large company allows a person to set up a business using their name and selling their goods. The company provides the products like hamburgers and french fries, does the advertising, and makes sure the individual franchises all do their business the company way. The owner of the franchise pays a fee to get started and a small part of the profits afterward.

SERVICE INDUSTRIES

Manufacturing industries create the most wealth and are expanding, but they employ far fewer people than 40 years ago because many of the jobs have been automated. Today 68 percent of working people are employed in service industries, such as shops, restaurants, garages, insurance offices, movies and television, and tourism.

The Hollywood area of Los Angeles is the center of the movie and television industry. The warm, sunny climate is ideal for making movies outdoors, and although that is not so important today because many movies are made on sets, Hollywood has remained the center of the industry. American movies and programs are shown all over the world, often with subtitles or dubbed into other languages. *E.T. the Extra-Terrestrial* is the all-time top American movie. It has made $229 million in the United States.

The tourist industry becomes more important as people have more leisure time.

The U.S. is a leader in designing and making miniaturized electrical circuits that are used in computers and computer-controlled machines. Many of these high-tech industries are located south of San Francisco in Silicon Valley.

The American space program put the first man on the moon and built the first space shuttle. The space shuttle goes into orbit like a rocket and then returns to Earth like an aircraft. The photo shows the space shuttle Discovery being launched from Cape Canaveral in Florida.

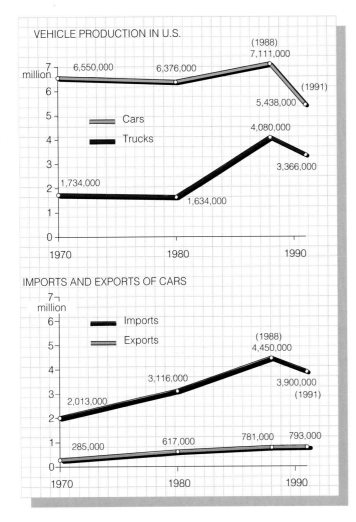

VEHICLE PRODUCTION IN U.S.

Cars
Trucks

6,550,000   6,376,000   (1988) 7,111,000   (1991) 5,438,000

1,734,000   1,634,000   4,080,000   3,366,000

IMPORTS AND EXPORTS OF CARS

Imports
Exports

2,013,000   3,116,000   (1988) 4,450,000   3,900,000 (1991)

285,000   617,000   781,000   793,000

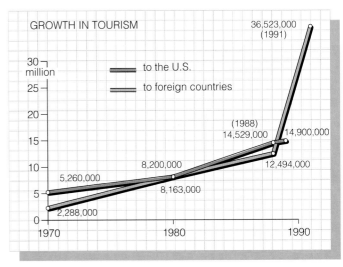

GROWTH IN TOURISM

to the U.S.
to foreign countries

36,523,000 (1991)

(1988) 14,529,000   14,900,000

5,260,000   8,200,000   12,494,000

2,288,000   8,163,000

One of the most popular places to visit in the U.S. is Florida, also known as the Sunshine State. Florida is very popular with northern tourists in winter. Along with the popular beaches of Miami, there are more than 20 or so major attractions around Orlando, including Disney World and Universal Studios, two of the most famous theme parks in the world. Disney World has over 14 million visitors a year from the U.S. and other countries.

The U.S. is becoming a popular destination for tourists from overseas because the cost of air travel has fallen. Of the 12.5 million overseas visitors, 5.5 million come from Western Europe. Florida is one of the most popular destinations.

Visitors to the U.S. spend about $34 billion a year, but this is just about equaled by the amount that American tourists spend abroad. Europe is the most popular foreign destination, receiving about 7 million American tourists a year.

AMERICAN TRADE

The U.S. has become a major trading country. The U.S. earns more money from the goods it exports than any other country, averaging around $320 billion a year. However, it spends far more on buying imports than it earns from exports and has the largest TRADE DEFICIT in the world at around $140 billion. Japan has the largest TRADE SURPLUS with the U.S. and is investing a lot of this money in American businesses. Japanese companies now own many American businesses as well as real estate.

Americans trade with Canada, Japan, Mexico, Great Britain and West Germany. Cars, mainly from Japan and Europe, account for 15 percent of all the manufactured goods that are imported. Other imports include televisions, radios, sound and video systems, and electronic goods. The manufactured goods exported

▶ Shares in American companies are traded at the Stock Exchange on Wall Street in New York. With London and Tokyo, it is one of the three big stock exchanges.

include computer and office equipment, aircraft, and motor vehicles.

WOMEN IN THE WORK FORCE

The number of women who go out to work has doubled over the past 30 years. Women now make up half the work force. However, they generally earn less than men even when they are doing similar jobs. There are very few women at the top of the big companies, but women are doing jobs that traditionally have only been done by men. For example, in 1975 all airline pilots were men. Today, one in 20 is a woman. There are also more women working as economists, lawyers, judges, and computer programmers.

The U.S. is so big that transportation is extremely important. About 10 percent of the work force is employed in the transportation industry.

Boats and barges moving around the coast, along the Mississippi River system, and across the Great Lakes were the earliest ways of moving large quantities of goods. Water transportation is still important today. It accounts for 37 percent of all freight carried. New Orleans, at the end of the Mississippi, is the largest port, handling over 193 million tons a year.

The railroads were built across the country to help the development of the West. They carried goods and people, but today they are mainly used to carry bulky goods, such as coal and wheat. Railroads account for 27 percent of freight carried. The rail network is 172,790 miles (278,245 km) long, the second largest in the world after Russia. The main railroad company is Amtrak.

▲ *The U.S. is a large country, and goods have to be carried great distances. Trains can be over a half mile long.*

There are about 42 million trucks in the U.S., and they carry 19 percent of the freight. Some are very large and carry goods very long distances. There is an excellent road system with 2.4 million miles (3.8 million km) of roads.

The U.S. needs a good road network because Americans are great travelers and go almost everywhere by car. The towns and the

KEY FACTS

● Eighty percent of downtown Los Angeles is devoted to the car, such as roads, parking places, and garages.
● In Los Angeles there are 90 cars for every 100 people old enough to drive.

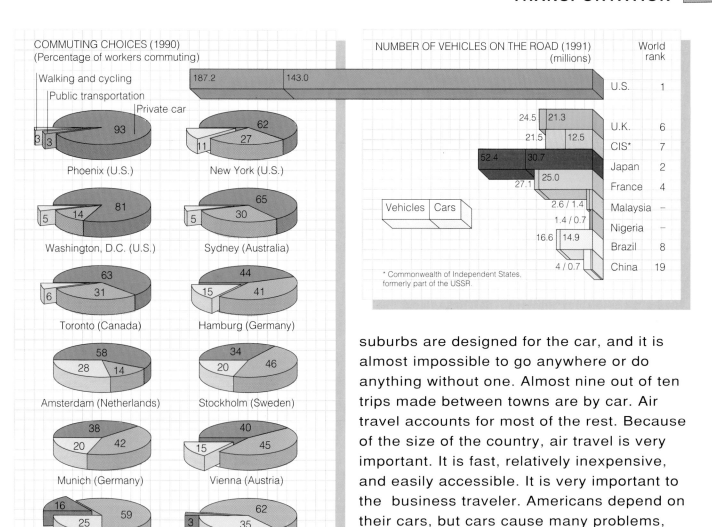

COMMUTING CHOICES (1990)
(Percentage of workers commuting)

- Walking and cycling
- Public transportation
- Private car

Phoenix (U.S.): 3 | 3 | 93

New York (U.S.): 11 | 27 | 62

Washington, D.C. (U.S.): 5 | 14 | 81

Sydney (Australia): 5 | 30 | 65

Toronto (Canada): 6 | 31 | 63

Hamburg (Germany): 15 | 41 | 44

Amsterdam (Netherlands): 28 | 14 | 58

Stockholm (Sweden): 20 | 46 | 34

Munich (Germany): 20 | 42 | 38

Vienna (Austria): 15 | 45 | 40

Tokyo (Japan): 25 | 59 | 16

Hong Kong: 3 | 35 | 62

NUMBER OF VEHICLES ON THE ROAD (1991)
(millions)

Country	Vehicles / Cars	World rank
U.S.	187.2 / 143.0	1
U.K.	24.5 / 21.3	6
CIS*	21.5 / 12.5	7
Japan	52.4 / 30.7	2
France	27.1 / 25.0	4
Malaysia	2.6 / 1.4	–
Nigeria	1.4 / 0.7	–
Brazil	16.6 / 14.9	8
China	4 / 0.7	19

Vehicles | Cars

* Commonwealth of Independent States, formerly part of the USSR.

suburbs are designed for the car, and it is almost impossible to go anywhere or do anything without one. Almost nine out of ten trips made between towns are by car. Air travel accounts for most of the rest. Because of the size of the country, air travel is very important. It is fast, relatively inexpensive, and easily accessible. It is very important to the business traveler. Americans depend on their cars, but cars cause many problems, especially traffic congestion and air pollution in the main cities.

▶ *The Bay Area Rapid Transit system (BART) was built to ease congestion on San Francisco's roads. The 7 mile (11 km) journey from Oakland takes 9 minutes instead of 40 minutes by road in the rush hours.*

THE ENVIRONMENT

The American way of life has many benefits, but it sometimes causes serious environmental problems. Americans have begun to seriously consider doing something to solve these problems. Sewage and chemicals from factories are killing wildlife in rivers. Large cities are regularly enveloped in smog. Cities are taking up more and more land. Mines are damaging the landscape, and farmers are turning more and more wildlife areas into farmland.

GARBAGE

Americans are the world's major consumers. They are also the major producers of garbage. Every day, each person produces about 4 pounds (1.8 kg) of garbage, such as paper, bottles, and glass. The amount doubled between 1960 and 1988 to almost 193 million tons a year. Although it contains valuable raw materials, most of the garbage is buried or burned. Only 14 percent is recycled.

AIR POLLUTION

Air pollution is a serious problem especially in and near big cities. Polluted air is unhealthy for people to breathe and damages buildings and wildlife. Pollution

▲*Dawn over Los Angeles and the haze caused by pollution is clearly visible. In 1989 the air was considered unhealthy to breathe on 206 days.*

can be carried hundreds of miles in the wind and fall as acid rain. Acid rain has killed wildlife in a quarter of the lakes in the Adirondack Mountains of New York State.

WATER POLLUTION

Sewage and industrial chemicals pollute some rivers and coastal waters. In 1969 the Cuyahoga River in Ohio was so full of oil, chemicals, and debris that it caught fire. Laws were passed in the 1970s to prevent

QUANTITIES OF POLLUTANTS PUT INTO ATMOSPHERE (1980s)
(thousands of tons)

HC 25,300	CO_2 83,710	NO_x 22,330	SO_x 26,290	U.S.
			1,474 / 1,385	
2,465	5,499	2,490	5,320	Japan*
2,169	7,282	2,817	3,862	U.K.
				France
		42 / 62 / 98 / 97		New Zealand

HC Hydrocarbons NO_x Nitrogen oxides
CO_2 Carbon dioxide SO_x Sulfur oxides
*HC and CO_2 figures not available

KEY FACTS

● Ninety percent of gasoline sold in the U.S. is unleaded.
● Only 1% of the plastics used in the U.S. are recycled.
● The U.S. produces 19% of all the world's garbage.
● Americans use 80 billion aluminum cans a year — 16 cans for every person in the world.
● More than three million people a year visit Yosemite National Park.
● Ninety percent of old growth forest in the northwest has been chopped down.

water pollution, but they are not always being obeyed. Some cities on the East Coast still pump untreated sewage into the sea. Pollution damages fish and other animals in the sea. One-third of the oyster beds off Louisiana and half of the shellfish beds of Texas have had to be closed because the food from them is too poisonous to eat.

WILDLIFE AT RISK

Large areas of the U.S. have been changed by farming, lumbering, and building. Every year 2.5 million acres (1 million ha) of land are taken over for roads, towns, and industry. As a result, there are fewer natural areas for wild plants and animals to live.

▲ **Yosemite National Park covers 1,188 square miles (3,061 sq km) in central California. It has spectacular scenery and many lakes, rivers, and waterfalls.**

For example, the prairies were once home to 60 million buffalo, but hunting, ranching, and grain farming reduced them to 300 by 1890. Wetland areas are particularly valuable for wildlife, but excluding Alaska, 75 percent of these areas have been destroyed by farming or other uses.

Many species of wildlife are in danger of becoming extinct, including America's national bird, the bald eagle. In 1991, 216 species of animals and 180 species of plants were on the endangered species list.

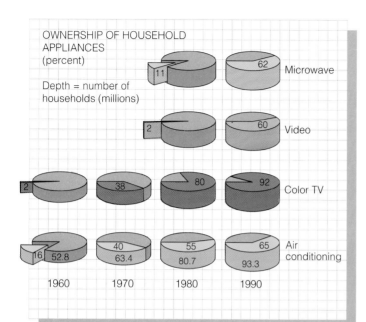

OWNERSHIP OF HOUSEHOLD APPLIANCES
(percent)

Depth = number of households (millions)

11	62			Microwave
	2	60		Video
2	38	80	92	Color TV
16 52.8	40 63.4	55 80.7	65 93.3	Air conditioning
1960	1970	1980	1990	

CONSUMER SPENDING PER HEAD 1988 (dollars)

Country	Dollars
U.S.	12,233
Japan	11,126
U.K.	7,396
USSR	2,280
France	9,635
Malaysia	815
Nigeria	621
Brazil	1,469
China	217

SOIL DAMAGE

Farmers depend on the soil, but since farming began in the U.S. one-third of the topsoil has been lost. Keeping too many cattle on ranges, removing forests from slopes, growing the same crop year after year, and dry weather conditions have created conditions in which the wind and rain can carry away the soil. Sometimes when irrigation is used, the hot weather brings salts to the surface of the soil. Plants cannot grow where the salts are found, so the soil becomes useless.

PROTECTION FOR THE ENVIRONMENT

Today, Americans are very well informed about environmental problems, and many belong to environmental organizations that are trying to protect the environment. The National Wildlife Federation has 5.8 million members, Greenpeace USA 2.3 million members, and the Sierra Club 633,000.

One way of protecting beautiful scenery and wildlife is to set up national parks where people are not allowed to live and there are no factories, major roads, or airports. Hunting is forbidden. Yellowstone in the Rockies was the world's first national

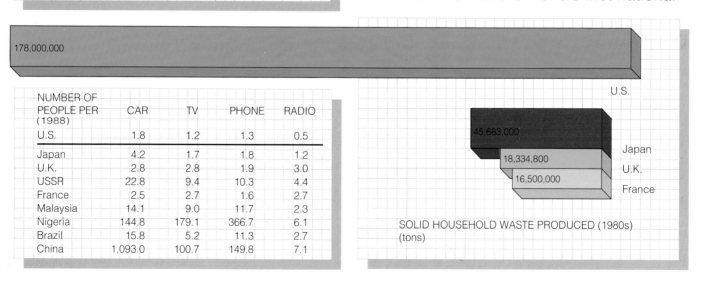

NUMBER OF PEOPLE PER (1988)	CAR	TV	PHONE	RADIO
U.S.	1.8	1.2	1.3	0.5
Japan	4.2	1.7	1.8	1.2
U.K.	2.8	2.8	1.9	3.0
USSR	22.8	9.4	10.3	4.4
France	2.5	2.7	1.6	2.7
Malaysia	14.1	9.0	11.7	2.3
Nigeria	144.8	179.1	366.7	6.1
Brazil	15.8	5.2	11.3	2.7
China	1,093.0	100.7	149.8	7.1

178,000,000 — U.S.
45,683,000 — Japan
18,334,800 — U.K.
16,500,000 — France

SOLID HOUSEHOLD WASTE PRODUCED (1980s)
(tons)

park. It was set up in 1872. Yellowstone is the largest national park in the U.S. There are 38 parks now, but many, such as Yosemite in California, have become so popular that they are getting overcrowded. Today cars are only allowed in certain parts of the parks. Campsites have to be booked in advance, and the number of hikers allowed on the trails is controlled.

The government has set up the Environmental Protection Agency. The EPA is helping to make and enforce environmental laws. Individual states also make their own laws.

Pollution is being controlled, and the quality of the air is slowly improving. For example, the quantity of carbon monoxide going into the air fell from 88 million tons in 1980 to 67 million tons in 1989. New cars create much less pollution than older models. Where there is strip mining the land has to be restored when the minerals are removed. In California, building on agricultural land is being prevented to stop the cities from spreading. Programs to recycle paper, glass, and metals are becoming more popular. In 1960 only 18 percent of old paper and 1.5 percent of glass were recycled. By 1988, these figures had risen to 26 percent for paper and 12 percent for glass.

▼*Many people feel strongly that more should be done to protect the environment. This is an Earth Day demonstration in New York City.*

THE FUTURE

The United States is one of the richest and most powerful countries in the world. Americans continue to plan for prosperity and power in the future.

The U.S. suffers from the same social and economic problems that exist in most industrialized countries, including poverty, drugs, and crime. More attention must be paid to the environment and conservation.

▶ *The bald eagle is a symbol of the U.S. Although hunting and pesticide poisoning almost made it extinct, conservationists are now protecting it.*

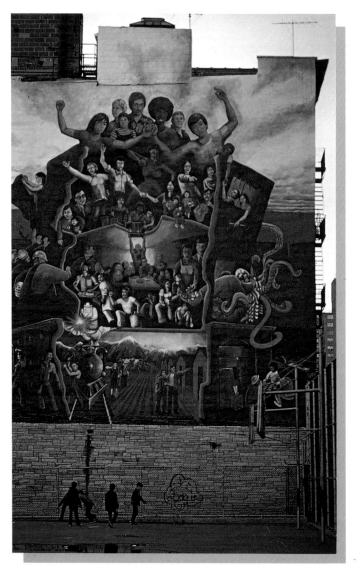

◀ *This painting on a wall in an inner city looks forward to a time when all people can live together in peace and harmony.*

Also, new jobs need to be created as automation replaces jobs, and American industry finds it difficult to compete with industries abroad. But the American reputation for hard work and creative solutions to problems offers hope.

Many countries are opposed to American policies. However, they also expect the U.S. to use its wealth and influence to help solve many of the world's problems. The United States has a great responsibility to the world and its people.

KEY FACTS

● The number of people living to over 100 is expected to rise from 56,000 in 1990 to 266,000 in 2020 — a fivefold increase.
● Spending on the environment is likely to increase from $19 billion a year in 1987 to $32 billion a year in 2000.

FURTHER INFORMATION

THE STATES OF THE U.S.

STATE	DATE OF STATEHOOD	CAPITAL	AREA (SQ MI)	POPULATION
Alabama	1819	Montgomery	51,705	4,062,608
Alaska	1959	Juneau	591,000	551,947
Arizona	1912	Phoenix	114,000	3,677,985
Arkansas	1836	Little Rock	53,187	2,362,239
California	1850	Sacramento	158,705	29,839,250
Colorado	1876	Denver	104,090	3,307,912
Connecticut	1788	Hartford	5,018	3,295,669
Delaware	1787	Dover	2,044	668,696
Florida	1845	Tallahassee	58,664	13,003,362
Georgia	1788	Atlanta	58,910	6,508,419
Hawaii	1959	Honolulu	6,471	1,115,274
Idaho	1890	Boise	83,564	1,011,986
Illinois	1818	Springfield	57,871	11,466,682
Indiana	1816	Indianapolis	34,413	5,564,228
Iowa	1846	Des Moines	56,275	2,787,424
Kansas	1861	Topeka	82,276	2,485,600
Kentucky	1792	Frankfort	40,409	3,698,969
Louisiana	1812	Baton Rouge	47,752	4,238,216
Maine	1820	Augusta	33,265	1,233,223
Maryland	1788	Annapolis	10,460	4,798,622
Massachusetts	1788	Boston	8,284	6,029,051
Michigan	1837	Lansing	97,102	9,328,784
Minnesota	1858	St. Paul	86,614	4,387,029
Mississippi	1817	Jackson	47,689	2,586,443
Missouri	1821	Jefferson City	69,697	5,137,804
Montana	1889	Helena	147,045	803,655
Nebraska	1867	Lincoln	77,355	1,584,617
Nevada	1864	Carson City	110,561	1,206,152
New Hampshire	1788	Concord	9,279	1,113,915
New Jersey	1787	Trenton	7,787	7,748,634
New Mexico	1912	Santa Fe	121,592	1,521,779
New York	1788	Albany	52,739	18,044,505
North Carolina	1789	Raleigh	52,669	6,657,630
North Dakota	1889	Bismarck	70,702	641,364
Ohio	1803	Columbus	44,787	10,887,325
Oklahoma	1907	Oklahoma City	69,956	3,157,604
Oregon	1859	Salem	97,073	2,853,733
Pennsylvania	1787	Harrisburg	46,043	11,924,710
Rhode Island	1790	Providence	1,212	1,005,984
South Carolina	1788	Columbia	31,113	3,505,707
South Dakota	1889	Pierre	77,116	699,999
Tennessee	1796	Nashville	42,144	4,896,641
Texas	1845	Austin	266,806	17,059,805
Utah	1896	Salt Lake City	84,898	1,727,784
Vermont	1791	Montpelier	9,614	564,964
Virginia	1788	Richmond	40,759	6,216,568
Washington	1889	Olympia	68,139	4,887,941
West Virginia	1863	Charleston	24,231	1,801,625
Wisconsin	1848	Madison	66,215	4,906,745
Wyoming	1890	Cheyenne	98,808	455,975

U.S. TRAVEL AND TOURISM ADMINISTRATION
Main Commerce Building, 14th Street and Constitution Avenue NW, Washington, D.C. 20230

UNITED STATES INFORMATION CENTER
301 4th Street SW, Washington, D.C. 20547

NATIONAL PARK SERVICE
1849 C Street NW, Room 1013, Washington, D.C. 20240

BOOKS ABOUT THE U.S.
Aten, Jerry. *Challenge Across America,* Good Apple, 1990
—— *Fifty Nifty States.* Good Apple, 1990
Aylesworth, Thomas G. *Kids' World Almanac of the United States.* Pharos, 1990
Carratello, John and Carratello, Patty. *Hooray for the USA!* Teacher Created Materials, 1991
Lancaster, Derek. *Picture America: States and Capitals.* Compact Classics, 1991
Shapiro, William, E., ed. *The Young People's Encyclopedia of the United States.* Millbrook, 1992

GLOSSARY

CAPITALISM
A way of life in which individuals own businesses and run them to try to make a profit

DEMOCRACY
A country which is governed by the politicians elected by the people of that country

DUBBED
When the language of the original dialogue is replaced by another language

MEGALOPOLIS
A large built-up area formed when several cities and towns spread out over the countryside and join up

STRIP MINING
Mining in which the land is stripped away to reach valuable minerals below the surface

TRADE DEFICIT
When the value of goods imported by a country is worth more than the value of goods exported. This is similar to people spending more money than they earn.

TRADE SURPLUS
When the value of goods exported by a country is worth more than the value of goods imported

INDEX

© Simon & Schuster Young Books 1992

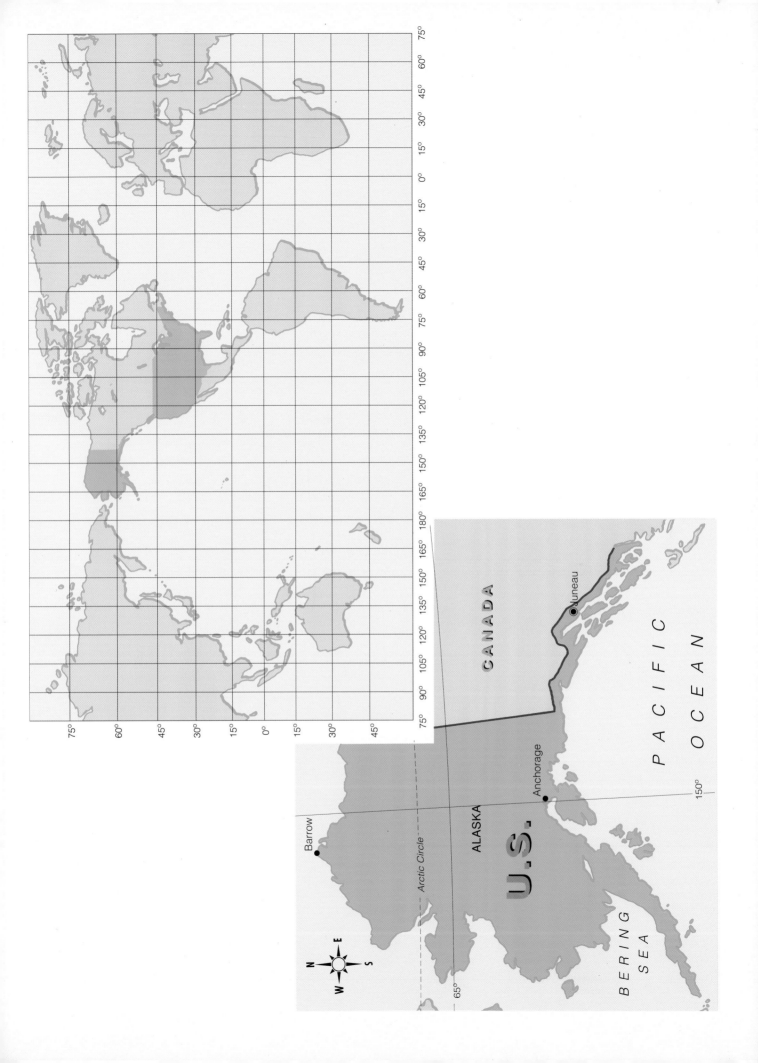

75°   60°   45°   30°   15°   0°   15°   30°   45°

75°   60°   45°   30°   15°   0°   15°   30°   45°   60°   75°

75°   60°   45°   30°   15°   0°   15°   30°   45°   60°   75°

CANADA

Juneau

PACIFIC OCEAN

Anchorage

ALASKA

U.S.

Barrow

Arctic Circle

65°

150°

BERING SEA

N
W   E
S